DISNEY

PIRATES of the CARIBBEAN

THE CURSE OF THE BLACK PEARL

Adapted by
IRENE TRIMBLE

Based on the screenplay by
TED ELLIOTT & TERRY ROSSIO and
screen story by TED ELLIOTT & TERRY ROSSIO
and STUART BEATTIE and JAY WOLPERT

Based on Walt Disney's
PIRATES OF THE CARIBBEAN

Produced by
JERRY BRUCKHEIMER

Directed by
GORE VERBINSKI

Level 2

Retold by Diana Eastment
Series Editors: Andy Hopkins and Jocelyn Potter

Pearson Education Limited
Edinburgh Gate, Harlow,
Essex CM20 2JE, England
and Associated Companies throughout the world.

ISBN: 978-1-4058-8170-8

First published by Penguin Books Ltd 2007
This edition published 2008

13

Set in 11/14 Bembo
Printed in China
SWTC/13

Published by Pearson Education Ltd

Every effort has been made to trace the copyright holders and we apologise in advance for any
unintentional omissions. We would be pleased to insert the appropriate acknowledgement in any
subsequent edition of this publication

For a complete list of the titles available in the Pearson English Readers series, please visit
www.pearsonenglishreaders.com. Alternatively, write to your local Pearson Education office
or to Pearson English Readers Marketing Department, Pearson Education, Edinburgh Gate,
Harlow, Essex CM20 2JE, England

Contents

Introduction

"Yo ho, yo ho, a pirate's life for me,
Yo ho, yo ho, a pirate's life ..."

These are the words of a pirate song, and this is a story of pirates—and gold.

Elizabeth Swann, an English girl, is on a ship to the Caribbean with her father some time in the 1600s when she sees a boy in the water. Who is he? How did he get there? And why is he wearing a gold medallion?

Years later, pirates take Elizabeth from her home. Will Turner, the boy in the water, is now a young man. He follows with Jack Sparrow. Jack is a pirate, too, but he is different. He is angry. Will wants to find Elizabeth, but what does Jack want? And what is the curse of the pirate ship, the *Black Pearl*?

Pirates of the Caribbean: The Curse of the Black Pearl (2003) is a Disney movie. It is exciting and it is funny. This book tells the story.

In the movie, Johnny Depp plays Jack Sparrow, Orlando Bloom plays Will Turner, and Keira Knightley plays Elizabeth Swann. Geoffrey Rush plays the pirate captain Barbossa.

People love and hate. They fight and die. And this book is not the end of the story of the ghostly pirates of the Caribbean. Look for *Pirates of the Caribbean: Dead Man's Chest* ...

Chapter 1   The Ghost Ship

Sailors tell a story about a big, black pirate ship. They see it sometimes when the fog is thick. The ghostly pirates on the black ship can never leave it because the ship carries a curse.

But this is only a story. There aren't really any ghosts. Or are there?

◆

The *Dauntless* sailed slowly through the thick fog. It was a big ship, and it carried fifty guns and a hundred strong men.

Twelve-year-old Elizabeth Swann stood at the front of the ship. She was on her way to Port Royal in Jamaica. Her father was the new governor there.

"I'd like to meet a pirate," she thought. She remembered an old song:

"Yo ho, yo ho, a pirate's life for me,
Yo ho, yo ho, a pirate's life …"

Suddenly, a sailor called to her.

"Quiet, Miss!" he said. "Pirates sail this ocean. You don't want to call them to us."

"Mr. Gibbs!" Captain Norrington shouted at the old sailor. "Don't be afraid," he said to Elizabeth. "There aren't any pirates here today."

"I'm not afraid," said Elizabeth.

But she knew the stories about pirates and fog.

They looked down at the dark water. There was something there. What was it? Wood? A box?

"Look!" Elizabeth shouted to the captain.

"It's a man!" said Captain Norrington.

"No, it's not," said Elizabeth. "It's a boy. Quickly, quickly, help him! Somebody help him!"

Captain Norrington called to his men.

"Get him out!"

The men pulled the boy onto the *Dauntless*.

"Is he OK?" asked Elizabeth.

"Oh, yes, Miss," said one of the sailors. "He's fine."

"But where did he come from?" asked Elizabeth. "There's nothing out there. Only the ocean."

Nobody spoke. And then a big ship came out of the fog. Every man on it was dead.

The men ran to the side of the *Dauntless* and looked down at the water. Were there any more people there?

"Miss, you stay with the boy," the captain said to Elizabeth.

Elizabeth sat down next to the boy. He was about the same age as her—ten or maybe eleven. Slowly, his eyes opened.

"Hello," said Elizabeth. "My name is Elizabeth Swann."

"I'm Will. Will Turner."

And then he was asleep again.

Elizabeth watched him. Then she saw something inside his shirt. Something gold. Slowly, she took it from him. She looked at it carefully. It was a medallion and there, on the front, was a skull and crossbones!

"Oh!" she thought. "Will Turner, you're ... a pirate!"

When Captain Norrington came back, she quickly put the medallion under her dress.

"Did he speak?" he asked.

"His name is Will Turner," she answered.

Inside her dress, she felt the gold medallion.

She looked out at the ocean—and there, in front of her, was a big, black ship. And it had the skull and crossbones, too!

The black ship turned away. But Elizabeth was suddenly very afraid.

"Oh!" she thought. "Will Turner, you're … a pirate!"

Chapter 2   Port Royal

Elizabeth opened her eyes. She was in bed, in the Governor's House in Port Royal.

She looked at the gold medallion and smiled. Every day she thought about the medallion. And every day she thought about Will Turner. Was it really eight years?

She heard her father.

"Are you in bed? Get up now!"

Governor Swann came into the room.

"It's a beautiful day," he said. "And look—I have something for you!"

He gave Elizabeth a box. Inside, there was a beautiful new dress from London.

"You can wear it today," he said, "for Captain Norrington's party."

"Oh, him," said Elizabeth.

"He's a good man. And he likes you, you know. He likes you very much. And after today, he will be a commodore."

The governor left the bedroom and went back to his office.

Will Turner was there. He was now twenty years old and a big, strong young man.

"Mr. Turner," said the governor. "Good day."

"Good day," said Will.

"Do you have it?"

"Yes, sir. Here it is."

He gave the governor a long box. The governor opened it carefully. He took out a sword and smiled.

"Ah, very good! A fine job!"

He wanted to give the sword to the new Commodore Norrington.

"Thank you, sir," Will said.

Will looked up and saw Elizabeth. She looked beautiful in her new dress.

"Ah, Elizabeth!" the governor said. "A wonderful dress!"

But Elizabeth's eyes were on Will.

"Hello, Will," she said. "I thought of you last night. Do you remember that first day, on the ship?"

"Of course I remember, Miss Swann," said Will. "I can never forget that day."

He smiled at her.

The governor wasn't happy with this conversation.

"We have to go," he said to Elizabeth. "It's time."

He took Elizabeth's arm. Elizabeth smiled at Will.

"Goodbye, Mr. Turner," she said.

The governor and his daughter left the house and went out into the busy street.

She looked beautiful in her new dress.

Chapter 3   Captain Jack Sparrow

Captain Jack Sparrow looked at the ships in Port Royal. His boat was small and old. He wanted a new, bigger ship. He had no money, but that wasn't a problem. Jack Sparrow was a pirate, and he had a plan.

He looked at the *Dauntless* for a long time. It was a big ship with fifty guns. Then he saw the *Interceptor*. It was smaller, but faster.

He wanted it.

There were two sailors next to the *Interceptor*. Jack went to them.

"Hey, you can't come here," one of them said. He looked at Jack's old boat and laughed. "Who are you? And what's that?"

"That's my boat," said Jack.

He smiled at the man and looked carefully at the *Interceptor*. The man smiled back.

"I like your ship," Jack said.

"Yes, it's the fastest ship in the Caribbean."

"Really?" said Jack. "Isn't the *Black Pearl* the fastest ship?"

The sailor laughed. "Ghost stories are for children," he said.

"It isn't a story," said the other sailor to his friend. "I saw that ship."

He turned to Jack—but Jack wasn't there. He was on the *Interceptor*.

The sailors ran after him.

"What are you doing?" they shouted. "You can't go up there! What's your name?"

"Smith," Jack answered.

"And what are you doing in Port Royal, Mr. Smith?"

"I want one of these ships," Jack said.

The sailors thought about this.

♦

High above the harbor, Elizabeth stood with Commodore Norrington. It was a hot day, and her dress was very heavy.

"Look at the ships down in the harbor," she said. "They're beautiful."

"And you are more beautiful," said Commodore Norrington. "You're a fine woman." Elizabeth didn't say anything. "I hope …" he said. "I hope that one day you will marry me, Elizabeth."

"Marry?" Elizabeth said. "Marry you?"

She moved back, but she couldn't move easily in her new dress. Suddenly, she fell.

She fell down, down into the harbor below.

On the *Interceptor*, Jack and the two sailors saw everything. The sailors didn't move.

"Quick!" Jack said to them. "Aren't you going to help her?"

"But we can't swim!"

"Here," said Jack. "Take these and don't lose them!"

He gave them his hat and his gun.

Jack jumped into the water and swam to Elizabeth. She was under the water. He took her hand and tried to help her. But her dress was too heavy!

Jack found his knife and cut the dress off. Then he pulled the young woman out.

Commodore Norrington and Governor Swann ran down to the harbor.

"Thank you! Thank you!" said the governor. "Elizabeth, my dearest daughter, are you OK?"

"Yes, yes, I'm fine," said Elizabeth.

She sat up.

Norrington looked at Jack.

"Good man!" he said. "Thank you! Give me your hand."

Then he saw it—a white *P* on Jack's hand. "I know you," he said. "You're a pirate!" He looked at Jack carefully. "Your name is Jack Sparrow."

"Captain *Jack Sparrow, please,*" said Jack.

"*Captain* Jack Sparrow, please," said Jack.

"I don't see your ship ... *captain,*" said Norrington. "And you're a pirate."

"He wanted to take one of our ships." The sailors from the *Interceptor* were with them now.

Norrington looked at Jack and laughed. Then he turned to the sailors.

"Take him away!" he said. "Put him in chains. Now!"

The sailors put chains on Jack.

"You can't do that!" said Elizabeth. "Maybe he is a pirate, but he helped me."

Suddenly, Jack moved. He jumped behind Elizabeth and put his chains around her.

The sailors showed their guns.

"No, no, don't shoot!" shouted Norrington. "Be careful! He'll kill her."

Jack pulled Elizabeth back.

"I really don't like you," Elizabeth said to him.

"I helped you and now you're helping me," Jack said.

He smiled. Then, suddenly, he took the chains off Elizabeth and ran.

"Get him!" shouted Norrington. "Get him, now!"

"I really don't like you," Elizabeth said.

Chapter 4   In the Blacksmith's Store

Jack ran down one street and up the next. He turned left. He turned right. He ran and ran. Then he listened.

He couldn't hear the sailors. He was free! But he had the chains on his hands.

He saw a store and opened the doors. Then he went in, very carefully. It was dark, but he could see some swords and knives.

"Ah, a blacksmith's store," he thought. "I can use one of those knives."

He took one and started to cut the chains. It was hard work, and it hurt his hands. But after a minute or two the chains fell to the floor.

Suddenly, Jack heard a sound behind him. It was Will Turner.

"What are you doing here?" asked Will. He looked at Jack. "Oh, you're the pirate. People are looking for you."

He took a sword.

"Is that a good idea?" asked Jack.

Will didn't speak. He put up his sword and looked at Jack.

They fought. Jack was quick, but Will was quick, too.

"You can use a sword!" said Jack.

He turned and ran to the door. But Will was too quick for him. He threw his sword at the door. It went over Jack's head. Jack tried to pull it out, but he couldn't. And now he couldn't open the door.

He turned to Will and smiled.

"That was good," he said. He looked at the other door to the store. "But you're between me and that door. And now you have no sword!"

Will took another sword and they fought again.

"Do you make these swords?" Jack asked.

"Yes, and I use them for three hours a day after work, too," Will answered.

"Why don't you find a girl? It's more exciting," Jack said. He took out a gun. "Now, move away from the door," he said.

Behind Jack, Will saw his boss, Mr. Brown. In Mr. Brown's hand there was a bottle. Slowly, the blacksmith moved his arm up. And then he hit Jack on the head—hard.

Jack fell to the ground.

Norrington arrived with his sailors. He looked down at Jack.

"Good work, Mr. Brown. Remember this day. On this day Captain Jack Sparrow *almost* got away!"

Mr. Brown looked at the glass on the ground.

"He broke my bottle!" he said.

Chapter 5   Pirates in Town

It was night, and there was a thick fog in Port Royal. Through the fog came a ship—a tall, black ship. It carried the skull and crossbones.

In her bed in the Governor's House, Elizabeth tried to read. She couldn't sleep. She saw the fog, and she thought about the pirates and the ghost story.

Down in the town, Will left the store and stood in the street. Everything was quiet—too quiet.

In his cell, Jack sat and thought. What could he do? How could he get out of this place? He looked out at the harbor and at the fog, but he wasn't afraid.

Suddenly, there was a loud noise from guns.

"I know those guns," Jack thought. "It's the *Pearl*!"

He heard the guns again. And again. Jack looked down at the town. It was on fire! Smoke came from the houses and the stores. People ran out into the streets.

And then, out of the smoke and the fog, the pirates came. They ran through the town, with their guns and their swords and their knives. They started more fires, and carried things away from the houses.

Will ran back into the store and took a sword and a knife. Then he went outside again.

"Elizabeth," he thought. "I have to help Elizabeth."

He started to run to the governor's house. But he didn't see the man behind him. The pirate hit him, hard, on the head, and Will fell to the ground.

Upstairs in her room, Elizabeth looked out her window and saw the fire and the smoke in the town. Then she looked down and saw two pirates at the door of the house. What could she do? Where could she go?

One of the pirates looked up. Ragetti was very dirty, and he only had one good eye. With it, he saw Elizabeth.

"Look, Pintel," he said. "Up there!"

Pintel looked up and smiled.

The pirates ran up the stairs. Elizabeth was afraid and quickly closed her bedroom door. The pirates hit the door, again and again. After some time, they broke the door and went into the room. But they couldn't see Elizabeth.

Suddenly, Elizabeth ran past them and out of the room.

She ran down the stairs and into the dining-room. The pirates ran after her. She looked for a gun, for a sword, but there was nothing there. She heard the pirates on the stairs. Where could she go?

There was a small closet at the back of the room. She went in and closed the door, very quietly.

The pirates came into the room.

"Come out, little girl," called Pintel. "You have something, and we want it."

"The gold is calling to us," said Ragetti. "Come out."

In the closet, Elizabeth didn't move. She had the gold medallion in her hand.

And then, suddenly, the door opened, and there was Ragetti. His one eye looked at her.

"Hello, little girl ..."

Chapter 6   On the *Black Pearl*

The pirates took Elizabeth to the *Black Pearl* in a small boat. When they climbed out, a man came out of the fog.

"Good day," he said to Elizabeth. "My name is Barbossa. I'm the captain of the *Black Pearl*."

Elizabeth looked around her. There were pirates everywhere. She was afraid, but she didn't show it.

"I am Elizabeth Turner." She didn't want to use her name. "I want you to leave Port Royal," she said. "Leave and never come back."

The pirates laughed.

"I'm sorry," said Barbossa. "But that isn't possible. We're looking for ..."

"I know!" shouted Elizabeth. She ran to the side of the boat and then showed them the gold medallion. "You're looking for this! Come near me and I'll throw it in the water."

The pirates didn't speak. Their eyes were on the medallion.

"I know you want it," said Elizabeth. "I know this ship. After eight years, I remember it. Now go and never come back!"

The pirates watched her, carefully. Elizabeth tried again. With the medallion in her hand, she looked down at the water.

"I'll throw it away now ..."

"OK, OK," said Barbossa. "You win. Give me the medallion, and we'll leave."

Elizabeth gave him the gold medallion.

"Stop the guns!" shouted Barbossa. "We're leaving." He looked at Elizabeth. "And, Miss Turner, you're going to come with us."

"But you have to take me back!" Elizabeth said.

"I'll throw it away now ..."

"No," said the pirate, and he smiled. "I stopped the guns, and we're going. But I'm not going to take you home. You're going to stay with us!"

Chapter 7   On the *Dauntless* and the *Interceptor*

When Will Turner woke up, his head hurt. But he thought only of Elizabeth. He ran to the governor's office.

He found the governor, Norrington, and the two sailors.

"The pirates have Elizabeth!" he shouted.

Norrington looked at him.

"Mr. Turner," he said. "You're a blacksmith. This isn't your fight. Please go."

"We have to find her," Will said.

"Of course we do," Norrington said. "And we will."

"Jack Sparrow!" said one of the sailors. "He knows about the *Black Pearl*."

"Go to Sparrow. Ask him!" shouted Will. "We can follow the ship! He can take us to it."

"Mr. Turner," said Norrington. "Please leave us. Now!"

He turned away.

Will ran to Jack's cell.

"Hey, you! Sparrow! Do you know the pirate ship—the *Black Pearl*?"

"Yes ..." said Jack.

"Where does it go?"

"It sails from the *Isla de Muerta*—the Island of the Dead. You know the stories. But why ask me?"

"They took Miss Swann," said Will angrily.

The pirate smiled.

"Oh, so you *did* find a girl ..." he said. "But what can I do? I'm in here."

"I can help you," said Will. "I can get you out of here, and then you can help me!"

Jack Sparrow thought about this.

"What's your name, boy?" he asked.

"Turner. Will Turner."

"Turner? OK, Mr. Turner. I'll help you. But first, I have to get out of this cell."

Will smiled. He was a blacksmith. He could open a cell door!

When Jack was free, he and Will went down to the harbor.

"What are we going to do?" asked Will.

"We're going to take that ship," said Jack. "The *Dauntless*."

"Take it? You're crazy!"

But Will followed Jack. The two men swam to the ship and climbed up the side. There were sailors on the ship.

"Don't move!" Jack told them. "I have a gun! I want this ship."

The sailors looked at Jack, then at Will. They started to laugh.

"But this is a big ship," one of them said. "You can't sail it with two men!"

"We can try," said Jack. "Now, leave!"

The sailors looked at Jack and Will. They looked at the gun. And then they got into a small boat and left the *Dauntless*.

From the *Interceptor*, Norrington saw Will and Jack on the *Dauntless*.

"What?" he thought. "You? But how ...? And where are you going on my ship?"

He turned to his sailors.

"Quickly," he said. "We have to catch the *Dauntless*. Now!"

The *Interceptor* was a faster ship, and minutes later it was near the *Dauntless*.

"Let's take them!" shouted Norrington.

He and his men went onto the *Dauntless*. Only one man stayed on the *Interceptor*.

Norrington's men looked everywhere.

"Where are you going on my ship?"

"Find them! I know they're here!" the captain shouted.

But Jack and Will weren't on the *Dauntless*. They were now on the *Interceptor*.

"Hello," said Jack to the only sailor there.

The man looked at him. He looked at Jack's sword. And he looked at Jack's gun.

"Can you swim?" asked Jack.

"Like a fish," said the sailor.

"Good!" said Jack and threw him in the water.

Commodore Norrington and his men saw the sailor when he fell.

"Stop them!" Norrington shouted. "Stop them!"

But it was too late. The *Interceptor* sailed out of the harbor.

Chapter 8   Dinner with Barbossa

Elizabeth sat at a table on the *Black Pearl*. There was a lot of food on the table—bread, fruit, and meat. Captain Barbossa sat at the other end of the table.

"Are you hungry?" he said. "Please eat."

Elizabeth was very hungry. She took some bread and some meat and started to eat.

"Have a drink," said Barbossa.

Elizabeth drank. Then she looked at the captain.

"You're not eating!" she said. "Is something wrong with the food? Are you trying to kill me? You eat it!"

She gave the captain some bread, but he didn't take it.

"I can't eat it," Barbossa said unhappily. "I'd like to. I'd love to. But I can't."

He took the gold medallion from his coat.

"This gold, Miss Turner, is very old. The Aztecs gave it to Cortés when he arrived in the Americas. There are many, many more of these. And the Aztecs put a curse on them.

"We found the gold on the *Isla de Muerta*," said Barbossa. "We took all of it. We bought food and drink with it. But then, suddenly, we couldn't eat and we couldn't drink. When we took the money, Miss Turner, the curse came with it."

The captain suddenly looked happier. "But now we can end the curse. We had to find all of the gold. Then we had to put it back on the island and give some blood. For ten years we looked for the gold on every ship and in every town ..."

"And now you have all of it," Elizabeth said.

"Yes. With this gold medallion, we have all of it. Thank you."

She thought for a minute.

"You have everything, and you're going to be free of the curse. So why am I here?"

"There's one more thing. You're Elizabeth Turner, the daughter of the pirate Bill Turner. He was one of us, but he isn't with us now. We have to have your blood!"

Elizabeth didn't understand, but she was afraid. Her blood?

She jumped up and tried to run. But Barbossa stood in front of her. She took a knife and pushed it into him. Then she ran outside. She closed her eyes. Her blood! What could she do?

She opened her eyes and saw the pirates at work. Then she looked carefully. They weren't men—they were skeletons!

Barbossa was behind her.

"Now, Miss Turner, you can really see us." He smiled. "Yes, Miss Turner, we're all ghosts. You're in a ghost story!"

Chapter 9   The Island of Tortuga

Will helped Jack on the *Interceptor*. The weather was good, and the wind was strong.

"You're not a sailor," said Jack. "You're a blacksmith. Where did you learn about sailing?"

"I worked on a ship when I was a boy," said Will. "I came from England. I wanted to find my father—Bill Turner."

"Is that right?"

"You knew my father," said Will. "I asked for your help when you were in the cell. You weren't interested. But when you heard my name, you said yes."

"Oh, I knew him," said Jack. "Everybody knew Bill. He was a good man. He was … a good pirate."

"No!" shouted Will. "You're wrong. My father wasn't a pirate."

He pulled out his sword.

"Put that away," Jack told him. "Why are you getting excited? Your father was a pirate, Mr. Turner. A good man, but a pirate. Now help me with this ship."

They arrived at the island of Tortuga.

"My father wasn't a pirate."

Tortuga was a small, dirty place. It had a harbor, some houses, an old store, and four bars. Bad men and pirates went there. They wanted to drink and to find women.

"Come with me," Jack said to Will. "We have to find some sailors for our ship."

They went into a bar and found an old man. His name was Joshaemee Gibbs. He was asleep, and he had a bottle in his hand. Jack kicked him.

"Wake up, Mr. Gibbs. We have work for you."

Slowly, Gibbs opened his eyes. "Oh, it's you. What do you want?"

Jack moved near to the old man. He didn't want Will to hear their conversation.

"We're looking for a ship," he said. "The *Black Pearl.*"

"The *Black Pearl?*" The old man sat up. "That's not smart, Jack Sparrow. You know the stories about the *Black Pearl.* Do you think Barbossa is going to give you his ship?"

Jack laughed. "Oh, I think he will," he answered. He looked at Will, and the old man's eyes followed his. "I have the boy and they want him."

"That boy?"

"The child of Bill Turner. His *only* child."

Joshaemee Gibbs didn't speak. He thought about Jack's words. And then he smiled.

"Ah, I understand," he said. "His only child. I think I can find some sailors for you now."

Gibbs did his job well. Some of the sailors were small; some were tall. Some were fat; some were thin. Some were smart; some were stupid. But they were all good sailors. They stood in front of their captain.

Jack looked at them. Then he showed them the ship.

"There's my ship, the *Interceptor*," he said. "It is a fine ship, a fast ship. Sail with me, and at the end you can have it! What do you say?"

The sailors shouted, "Yes!"

Jack stopped in front of a sailor in a very big hat. Suddenly a hand came out from under the hat and hit him. Jack fell to the ground. The hat fell, too—and showed a woman's face.

Jack stood up.

"Hello, AnaMaria," he said.

"You took my boat!" she shouted.

"Ah ..." said Jack slowly.

"And where is it now? Do you have it?"

"No, I don't. But this ship is better." He turned to the men. "Get ready!" he said. "We're going to sail. And AnaMaria will give you your work."

The sailors ran onto the ship, and the *Interceptor* left Tortuga.

Gibbs and Will sat and looked out at the ocean.

"Do you know Captain Sparrow well?" Will asked.

"Oh yes," said Gibbs. "I knew him when he was captain of the *Black Pearl*."

"What? Captain of the *Black Pearl*? But how …?"

"Listen to the story," said Gibbs. "Jack Sparrow was a pirate, but he was a good man. He found the *Isla de Muerta*—and there was gold for every sailor on his ship. But his sailors didn't want Jack Sparrow. They wanted the gold. So they left him on an island with no food and no water—only his gun."

"They left him?"

"They left him—but he got away. And now he wants to find those pirates, and he wants to use that gun. He wants to shoot their captain, Barbossa!"

♦

The *Black Pearl* was at the *Isla de Muerta*.

"It's time, my dear," said Ragetti.

He smiled at her, but his one good eye watched her carefully.

They put her in a small boat and left the *Black Pearl*. The fog got thinner.

Elizabeth could see a big, black cave.

"Are we going in there?" she asked.

"Yes, my dear," said Pintel.

Chapter 10 Gold!

A short time later, Will and Jack and their men arrived at the *Isla de Muerta*, too. Through the fog, they could see ships—old ships under the water.

Jack turned to Gibbs. "Stay here with the men," he said.

Jack and Will got into a smaller boat and started to go to the island.

"Do you see that?" said Will. "There! A cave, I think."

The boat moved slowly into the cave. It was very dark, and the walls were wet. Jack and Will didn't speak. On their left, they saw a light, and next to it was a skeleton. It had a sword in its back.

They stopped the boat and jumped out. Then Will followed Jack, and they climbed for a short time.

Suddenly, they saw some lights. In front of them was a second, bigger cave. They saw gold boxes, gold cups, gold plates, and gold swords. And a lot of money. The cave was full of gold!

In the middle of the cave, in the middle of the gold, Elizabeth stood next to an old Aztec box. She couldn't move because Barbossa had his hands on her.

Will wanted to go to her, but Jack stopped him.

"No!" he said. "We have to wait."

Will didn't want to wait. Elizabeth's life was too important to him.

"I'm sorry, Jack," he said, and he hit Jack hard.

Jack fell to the ground. He didn't move.

Will looked around the cave and listened.

"Do you know my plan?" Captain Barbossa said to his men. "When this curse ends, I'm going to eat fruit. A lot of fruit!"

The other pirates laughed.

Barbossa looked at Elizabeth. He took her hand and cut it with a knife. Then he put the medallion on her hand and closed her hand around it.

"Blood," he said. "Turner's blood. The curse started with blood and it ends with blood."

He took the bloody medallion from Elizabeth and put it into the box, onto the gold.

The pirates waited.

"I don't feel different," Ragetti said. "Is that really the end of the curse?"

"How will we know?" Pintel asked.

Barbossa thought about that. Then he took out his gun and shot Pintel. Pintel stayed on his feet.

The pirates were very unhappy.

"Oh, it didn't work!" they shouted.

The cave was full of gold!

Barbossa didn't understand.

"You!" he said to Elizabeth. "Was your father William Turner? Bill Turner?"

"No," she said.

The pirates shouted again.

"She's not Turner's child!"

"She's the wrong person!"

"But she had the medallion!"

"She's the right age."

They called to Barbossa.

"*You* killed Bill."

"*You* started this!"

Nobody looked at Elizabeth.

Suddenly, she felt a hand on her arm. It was Will.

"Come with me," he said quietly. "Quickly. Now."

Elizabeth started to move. But first, she took the medallion.

They ran to the boat.

"Look, the girl! She has the medallion! Get them!"

The pirates ran to their boats. Then they saw Jack.

"Jack Sparrow!" said Barbossa. "Aren't you dead?"

"No, I'm not dead."

"But you will be ..."

Barbossa took out his gun.

"Wait, wait," said Jack. "The girl's blood didn't work."

"How do *you* know?"

"I know. You don't want *her* blood. I can help you."

Chapter 11   The Blood of a Pirate

Will and Elizabeth arrived at the *Interceptor*.

"Where's Jack?" asked Gibbs.

"Yes, where's Jack?" asked AnaMaria.

Jack? Jack Sparrow? Elizabeth wasn't happy. She didn't want the help of a pirate.

"He's on the island," Will told them. "We have to go—now."

"OK," said Gibbs. "Get ready!" he shouted to the other sailors.

Will and Elizabeth went to the back of the boat. Will looked into Elizabeth's eyes. He moved nearer but Elizabeth stopped him.

"This is yours," she said.

She gave him the gold medallion.

"What's this?" he asked.

"Don't you remember? You had it when I found you."

"Oh yes," said Will. He looked at the medallion. "It was my father's." And then he understood. "They have to have *my* blood—not yours. My father's blood. The blood of a pirate!"

♦

Jack and Barbossa sat at a table on the *Black Pearl*.

"Ah, my ship," Jack said.

"It isn't your ship now," Barbossa said angrily.

"You give me my ship," Jack said, "and I'll give you a name. You'll have your blood. And I want to say thank you."

"Why?"

"You left me on that island," Jack said. "You took the gold, and the curse went with it. But the curse isn't on me. So thank you!"

A pirate came in.

"We can see the *Interceptor*," he said.

"Get the guns ready," shouted Barbossa.

"Why don't I go onto the ship and talk to them?" Jack said. "I'll get your medallion."

"No, you won't." Barbossa turned to his sailors. "Take him downstairs—and watch him!"

The *Black Pearl* moved faster and faster.

♦

The sailors on the *Interceptor* watched the pirate ship.

"It's too fast," Gibbs shouted.

"We're too heavy," said AnaMaria.

They threw everything into the water: boxes, bottles, food. But the *Black Pearl* was very near them now.

Then it was at their side.

The fight was short, and Barbossa's pirates quickly won. They took Elizabeth and Jack's sailors onto the *Black Pearl*.

Barbossa had the medallion in his hand.

Suddenly, Will was there in front of him! He had a gun.

"She goes free!" he said. "Elizabeth goes free."

They took Elizabeth and Jack's sailors onto the Black Pearl.

"No, she doesn't, boy," said Barbossa. "Put down that gun. You can't kill me. We're ghosts. We can't die."

"*You* can't. But *I* can." Will put the gun to his head. "My name is Will Turner. My father was Bill Turner. His blood is my blood!"

The pirates looked at Will. They didn't move.

"Without my blood," said Will, "the curse will always be with you."

He was right. The pirates knew it.

"OK, Mr. Turner," said Barbossa. "What do you want?"

"Elizabeth goes free."

"Yes. We know that. And?"

Will thought hard. This game was new to him.

"And ... and the sailors of the *Interceptor.*"

"OK," said Barbossa.

Will put down his gun. Barbossa took it and smiled.

"Jack and the girl will go to that island," he said.

He showed them a very small island near the boat.

"But they won't be free!" shouted Will. "You said ..."

"They *will* be free. But they'll be free on that island."

Chapter 12   On a Small Island

"Now," Barbossa said to Jack, "it's time for a swim."

"Last time you gave me a gun," said Jack.

"Yes, that's right." Barbossa turned to his sailors. "Give him his gun."

"There are two of us. We want two guns."

"Only one. You can shoot the girl with it."

Barbossa took the gun and threw it into the water. Elizabeth jumped in and Jack followed. They swam to the bottom and got the gun. Then they swam to the island.

They looked back at the *Black Pearl.*

"He has my ship again!" said Jack angrily. "For the second time!"

27

Elizabeth looked around the island.

"It's not very big," she said.

Jack didn't speak. He remembered this island. He sat down and started to make a fire.

"How can we get away?" asked Elizabeth.

"We can't."

"How long can we live here?"

"Oh, there's food on the trees. Maybe a month. Maybe more."

"But we don't have a month! We have to help Will! We have to do something now!"

Elizabeth sat by the fire and started to sing the old song:

"Yo ho, yo ho, a pirate's life for me,

Yo ho, yo ho, a pirate's life …

We drink, we fight, and then we die,

Yo ho, yo ho, and we drink to a pirate's life."

"How do you know that?" Jack asked.

"Oh, I learned it when I was a child."

"I love that song," said Jack.

He sang with her.

"We're hard and we're bad and we fight and we drink …"

And then he fell asleep.

Elizabeth thought hard. Then she started to work. She got more wood and put it on the fire. Then she found more and more wood.

When Jack woke up, there was fire everywhere.

"What are you doing?" he asked Elizabeth. "We have to live here!"

"Look at the smoke," Elizabeth said.

He looked. There was a lot of smoke.

"You see?" Elizabeth said. "Everybody is looking for us. And when they see the smoke …"

"Nobody will see it," Jack said. "They aren't looking around here."

Jack walked down to the water. And then he saw it—a ship! An English ship! It was the *Dauntless*.

"She's never going to forget this," he thought.

"We have to live here!"

Chapter 13   Back to the *Isla de Muerta*

Jack was on the *Dauntless* again. And again, Commodore Norrington wanted to put him in chains.

"Mr. Norrington!" Elizabeth said. "We have to go to the *Isla de Muerta*. Captain Sparrow can help us, but not in chains."

"Commodore Norrington," said Jack, "Barbossa is the captain of the last pirate ship in the Caribbean. You have to catch him. But without me, how can you find him?"

Norrington thought about this.

"We have to go back to Port Royal," he said. "The governor

29

wants to take his daughter home. We can't go after pirates."

"Please, please," said Elizabeth. "Will is on the *Isla de Muerta*. We have to help him."

"Do we?"

"Mr. Norrington, you want to marry me. We can marry. We will marry. But first, we have to help Will. Please do it for me."

Norrington smiled. Then he turned to his sailors.

"OK, men, get ready. We're going to the *Isla de Muerta!*"

◆

Will and the ghostly pirates were in the cave on the *Isla de Muerta*.

"It isn't a problem," Pintel told Will. "It's only a little blood."

"Maybe more than a little," said Barbossa.

He pushed Will down on the floor and put a knife to his head.

"Excuse me!"

"Who's that?" said Barbossa. "Who's there?"

"It's me. Captain Jack Sparrow."

Jack walked into the cave.

Barbossa looked at him.

"Not you again!" he said. "How did you get off the island?"

Jack laughed, and Barbossa got angry.

"First Turner, then you," he said to Jack. "I want to see you die."

"No," said Jack, very slowly. "You don't want to do that."

"And why not?"

"Because the *Dauntless* is here. They want to take you."

Barbossa took the knife away from Will's head.

"Take us? They can't. We're not men, we're ghosts."

"You're ghosts now. But after the blood? When you're men again, they can kill you."

Barbossa thought about this.

"So, what's your plan?" he said.

"Go out to the *Dauntless* now. Ghosts can take the *Dauntless*. Then you'll have two ships."

Barbossa took the knife away from Will's head.

"And what do *you* want?"

"I want to be a captain again. Under you, of course. You'll have the *Dauntless*, and I'll be your captain on the *Black Pearl*."

Barbossa smiled.

"OK. Let's do it!"

◆

Outside the cave, Commodore Norrington waited on the water. He had seven small boats and more than fifty men. It was time for a fight!

But when the ghostly pirates started to move, Norrington didn't see them. They weren't in their boats. They walked on the ocean floor, below Norrington and his men. Only the fish saw them.

"Where are they?" said one of the sailors. "Can anybody see them?"

Suddenly, they heard a loud noise. Guns! On the *Dauntless*! Commodore Norrington turned and looked at his ship. He saw his men. And he saw … skeletons.

"Quickly!" he shouted. "Back to the ship!"

They went back to the *Dauntless* and climbed up the side. They shot at the ghostly pirates, but they couldn't kill them. Then Norrington saw Governor Swann.

"Are you OK, sir?" he asked.

"I'm OK. But where's Elizabeth?"

Chapter 14   The End of the Curse

At the same time, Elizabeth left the *Dauntless* and swam to the *Black Pearl*. She climbed up the side and heard pirates. There were only two of them on the ship. They wanted Barbossa to come back. They wanted the end of the curse.

The sailors looked at the food on the captain's table.

"What will you eat first?" one asked.

"Cake. A lot of cake," said the other man.

Quietly, Elizabeth climbed onto the *Pearl*. But then the pirates saw her.

"Hey, you! Stop!"

Elizabeth ran and the pirates followed. But they stopped when they heard a noise behind them.

"What was that?"

"I …"

Gibbs was there. Then AnaMaria, and more sailors. They pushed the two pirates, hard, and the pirates fell into the water.

"Who are you?" said Elizabeth.

"We're Jack Sparrow's sailors," said one of them. "And now the *Black Pearl* is ours!"

"Good!" said Elizabeth. "We have to help Will. And Jack, too. Quick! We have to go into the cave."

But the sailors didn't move.

"No," said AnaMaria. "The *Black Pearl* is ours, not Jack Sparrow's. He took my boat."

"OK," said Elizabeth. "Then I'll go without you!"

♦

In the cave, Jack, Will, and Barbossa looked at the gold.

"I don't understand you," said Barbossa. "Are you with them or with us?"

"I'm a difficult man," said Jack. "Nobody understands me. Here, catch!" he said to Will, suddenly.

He threw a sword from the floor to the young man.

"Jack!" said Barbossa. "I almost liked you!"

Jack laughed.

"Remember, I am a pirate!" he said.

Jack fought Barbossa, and Will fought Barbossa's men.

Suddenly, Barbossa stopped.

Jack fought Barbossa.

"You can't win, Jack," he said.

Then he pushed his sword hard into Jack. It went through him and came out of his back.

Jack stopped fighting. Will stopped fighting. They looked at the end of the sword.

"I liked your curse," said Jack. "I wanted some gold, too."

He pulled a gold medallion from his pants. He was a skeleton, too!

Jack pulled the sword out, and the two skeletons fought again. Barbossa was good with a sword, but Jack was better and quicker. But ghosts don't die. He couldn't kill Barbossa, and Barbossa couldn't kill him.

Will fought the other pirates. Then, suddenly, he saw Elizabeth.

"I want to help you," she said.

She took a sword and started to fight.

But Barbossa saw Elizabeth, too. He put his sword near her head.

"I win, Captain Sparrow," he said. "Give me your sword, or the girl dies."

Jack didn't move. He looked at Elizabeth and then at Will. He took out his gun and looked at Barbossa. Then he shot Barbossa.

Barbossa smiled.

"Are you stupid? You wait ten years and then you use your gun on me. You can't kill me!"

"He's not stupid," said Will.

He stood next to the box of pirate gold with the medallion in his hand. His hand was bloody. He put the medallion in the box.

Barbossa stopped talking. He looked down at his shirt and saw blood. Then he fell down, dead.

At the same time, on the *Dauntless*, the other pirates changed, too. The skeletons were now men.

"What's happening?" said one of them. "I feel …"

Norrington's men fought them easily. Some pirates died.

The men put the other pirates in chains.

In the cave, Jack cut his hand. He put some blood onto his medallion and put the medallion in the box. He took some other gold from the floor. Then he left the cave with Elizabeth and Will. But the *Black Pearl* wasn't there.

He sat down.

"I'm sorry, Jack," Elizabeth said.

"I understand," said Jack. "I was late, so they didn't wait. They were right. Pirates don't wait for anybody."

Chapter 15 The Last of the Pirates

Jack stood in front of the governor, Commodore Norrington, Norrington's sailors, and people from the town.

"It's time, Jack Sparrow," said the governor. "You're a pirate, and now you have to die!"

"But Father!" shouted Elizabeth. "He's a good man. He helped me, and he helped your men."

"I know," said the governor. "But he's a pirate."

"You're a pirate, and now you have to die!"

Suddenly, Will was at Elizabeth's side. "I love you, Elizabeth," he said. "I wanted to tell you before, but I couldn't."

Then he ran to Jack and threw him a sword. They fought Norrington's men. Elizabeth and her father watched.

"Shoot Sparrow!" shouted Norrington. "Use your guns!"

Will stood in front of Jack.

"Shoot him, and you shoot me," he said.

"Will!" said the governor. "What are you doing? This man is a pirate!"

"And a good man!" Will shouted.

"You're nobody, Turner," said Norrington.

Will looked at him.

"I'm the man between you and Jack," he said.

Elizabeth stood next to Will.

"And my place is here, too!" she said.

Norrington looked from Will to Elizabeth. He knew now. She didn't love him. She loved Will.

Jack looked at the people around them.

"Friends," he said. "Remember this day. On this day you *almost* killed ..."

But he didn't finish. He fell back into the harbor.

Everybody ran and looked down. There, below them, they saw the *Black Pearl*. And on the *Black Pearl* were Jack's sailors. They were there for their captain.

Norrington looked at Will. Then he looked at his sword.

"This is a good sword," he said. "A good man made it. I hope you're a good man, Will Turner." He turned to Elizabeth. "I hope you two will be very happy, Miss Swann," he said.

A sailor ran to them.

"Commodore Norrington, sir, do we follow the *Black Pearl*?"

"Not now. I think we can give them some time. We'll follow them later."

He walked away.

They were there for their captain.

Will looked at Elizabeth and she smiled back at him.

"Oh dear," said the governor. "He isn't a sailor—he isn't a captain. He's only a blacksmith."

"He's a pirate!" said Elizabeth. She smiled again.

Jack swam to the *Black Pearl* and climbed onto the ship.

"You came for me!" he said to Gibbs.

Gibbs looked at the floor.

"I know it was wrong of us. But ..."

Jack smiled. He looked back at Port Royal. Then he looked out across the ocean. It was a beautiful day.

AnaMaria was at the front of the ship. She turned to him.

"Captain Sparrow," she said, "the *Black Pearl* is yours."

Jack took off his hat and his coat. Then he smiled and turned the boat to the east.

He started to sing:

"Yo ho, yo ho, a pirate's life for me ..."

ACTIVITIES

Chapters 1–3

Before you read

1 Look at the pictures in these three chapters. Answer these questions.
   a What is happening in each picture?
   b Which actors or people in the story can you name?
   c Will the story be:
      – funny or sad?
      – exciting or boring?
      – about love or hate?

2 Look at the Word List at the back of the book. Answer these questions.
   a What are the words in your language?
   b What do you know about pirates?
   c Do you know any other stories about a curse or about ghosts?
   d Are there any islands in your country? What is the name of the biggest island?
   e Are there any harbors? Where is the most important harbor?
   f Are there any caves? Can you go into them? What can you see there?

While you read

3 Which are the right words?
   a The *Dauntless is / isn't* a pirate ship.
   b Elizabeth sees *a man / a boy* in the water.
   c Elizabeth *wants / doesn't want* Norrington to see the medallion.
   d She sees a big *black / white* ship.
   e Norrington *likes / doesn't like* Elizabeth.
   f The governor is going to give Norrington *a box / a sword.*
   g The governor is *happy / unhappy* when Will smiles at Elizabeth.
   h Jack Sparrow wants to take the *Dauntless / Interceptor.*
   i Jack helps *Elizabeth / Norrington.*
   j Norrington sees a white *letter / number* on Jack's hand.

After you read

  4 Who are these people? What do you know about them?

     a Elizabeth Swann

     b Will Turner

     c Jack Sparrow

     d Norrington

  5 Answer these questions. Why:

     a is Will wearing a medallion with a skull and crossbones on it?

     b does Jack Sparrow want a new ship?

     c does Jack put his chains around Elizabeth?

  6 Talk about the pictures in chapters 1–3.

     a Who can you see in the picture?

     b What are they doing?

     c What are they saying?

Chapters 4–6

Before you read

  7 Discuss these questions.

     a Where will Jack go now? Do you think Norrington's men will catch him? Why (not)?

     b Do you think Elizabeth will marry Commodore Norrington? Why (not)?

While you read

  8 Are these sentences right (R) or wrong (W)?

     a Jack Sparrow sees gold in the blacksmith's store.   .....

     b Will Turner fights Jack.   .....

     c Mr. Brown hits Jack on the head with a bottle.   .....

     d There is fog in the harbor when the pirates arrive.   .....

     e The pirates only start one fire in Port Royal.   .....

     f A pirate kills Will.   .....

     g The pirates take Elizabeth.   .....

     h The pirate captain's name is Pintel.   .....

     i The pirates want the medallion.   .....

After you read

9 Who is talking? Who are they talking to?

    a "People are looking for you."

    b "You're between me and that door."

    c "He broke my bottle!"

    d "Come out, little girl."

    e "Come near me and I'll throw it in the water."

    f "You're going to stay with us!"

10 Work with another student. Have this conversation. You are on the *Black Pearl*.

    Student A: You are Elizabeth. You want the pirates to leave Port Royal—now. Tell Barbossa.

    Student B: You are Barbossa. You want Elizabeth, but you have to have the medallion, too.

Chapters 7–9

Before you read

11 Read the first twelve lines of Chapter 7. What do you think will happen next in the story?

While you read

12 Write a word in each sentence.

    a When Will wakes up, his head ....

    b He .... Commodore Norrington about the pirates.

    c Will .... Jack for his help.

    d He .... the cell door for Jack.

    e Will and Jack .... the *Dauntless* from the English sailors.

    f Norrington and his men .... the *Dauntless* on the *Interceptor*.

    g Will and Jack .... the *Interceptor* out of the harbor.

13 Who are they?

    a There is a curse on *them*.   ....

    b The pirates want *her* blood.   ....

    c *They* are really ghosts.   ....

    d *He* knows about Will's father.   ....

    e *He* was a good man, but he was a pirate.   ....

   f Jack took *her* boat.   ....

   g Barbossa left *him* on an island.   ....

After you read

14 Discuss these questions.

   a Why do the pirates think that they want Elizabeth?

   b Why do they really want Will?

   c What does Jack want? Why?

Chapters 10–12

Before you read

15 Discuss these questions.

   a What will Elizabeth see in the cave?

   b What will happen to her there?

While you read

16 What happens first? What happens next? Write the numbers 1–6.

   a Barbossa cuts Elizabeth's hand.   .....

   b Barbossa shoots Pintel.   .....

   c Will and Jack arrive at the *Isla de Muerta*.   .....

   d Elizabeth gives Will the medallion.   .....

   e Elizabeth and Will run to a boat.   .....

   f Will hits Jack hard.   .....

17 Which are the right words?

   a The *Black Pearl* is *faster / slower* than the *Interceptor*.

   b The pirates want Will because his father *was / wasn't* a pirate.

   c The pirates send Jack and Elizabeth to *the cave / an island*.

   d The sailors on the *Dauntless / Interceptor* see Elizabeth's fire.

After you read

18 Why are these things important in the story?

   a gold

   b fire

   c blood

19 Look at the pictures in chapters 10–12. Would you like to be one of the people in the cave, on the *Black Pearl*, or on the island? Why (not)? Tell the class.

Chapters 13–15

20 What will happen to these people at the end of the story? What do you think?

    a Elizabeth

    b Will

    c Jack

    d Commodore Norrington

    e Barbossa

While you read

21 Write the names.

    a Who puts a knife to Will's head? ....

    b Who wants to be the captain of the *Black Pearl* again? ....

    c Who climbs on to the *Black Pearl*? ....

    d Who pushes the two pirates into the water? ....

    e Who pushes a sword into Jack? ....

    f Who cuts his hand first and ends the curse? ....

    g Who dies first? ....

    h Who helps Jack in Port Royal? ....

    i Who is going to marry Elizabeth? ....

    j Who, at the end, is captain of the *Black Pearl*? ....

After you read

22 Have a conversation between Jack and a new friend after the end of the story.

    Student A: You are the friend. Ask Jack questions. Why is he a pirate? How did he get his ship? What is he going to do now?

    Student B: You are Jack. Answer your friend's questions.

23 Which people are unhappy at the end of the story? Why? Talk about their feelings.

Writing

24 Write a letter from Elizabeth to a friend the day after she found Will in the water.

25 When the curse ends, the pirates change from skeletons into men. Write a conversation between two of them before they die.

26 Write about one of the pictures in the book. What is happening? What happened before this? What is going to happen next?

27 At the end of the story, Jack Sparrow and his friends sail away from Port Royal. What are they going to do next? Write the story.

28 Write a letter from the governor to his brother in England. Write about Elizabeth and Will, and the governor's feelings about Will.

29 Would you like to be a pirate? What is good about a pirate's life, and what is bad? Write about it.

30 A lot of things happen in this story. Which is the most exciting? Why?

WORD LIST *with example sentences*

blacksmith (n) The *blacksmith* is making new shoes for my horse.

blood (n) He cut his hand, and there was *blood* everywhere. He is washing his *bloody* clothes now.

captain (n) When the *captain* speaks, everybody on the ship listens. But the captain has to listen to the **commodore**.

cave (n) Some animals live in *caves* in the mountains.

cell (n) The police caught the men with guns and put them into a *cell*.

chain (n) The police put *chains* around the man's hands and feet and took him away.

curse (n/v) In the story, a *curse* changed people into animals.

fog (n) We couldn't see anything through the thick *fog*.

ghost (n) Are there *ghosts* in this old building? I heard *ghostly* noises last night.

gold (n) People look for *gold* because they want to get rich quickly.

governor (n) When the *governor* has a party, the most important people go to it.

harbor (n) The men are in town because their ship is in the *harbor*.

island (n) They live on an *island* in the middle of the Atlantic Ocean.

medallion (n) The singer wears an expensive *medallion* under his shirt.

pirate (n) *Pirates* took the ship and killed everybody on it.

sail (v) Our friends are going to *sail* around the world in their new boat.

side (n) The child's ball hit the *side* of the house.

skeleton (n) The doctors studied *skeletons* when they were students.

skull and crossbones (n) There is a *skull and crossbones* on that ship. The men on the ship are very dangerous.

sword (n) Put the *sword* away. You are going to hurt somebody!